D0323765

To

From

Tish Suk has successfully practiced what she prescribes in her writings. Her personal life and family reflect the values she shares with us. Her words of wisdom are easy bite-sized nuggets that even the busiest person can digest.

Chris Herning, *high school pastor*

Tish has been coaching parents of teens and offering them solutions for years. Her practical wisdom equips them with positive, uncomplicated ways to accomplish what every parent wants: more connection with their teens. This collection of tips keeps the focus on strengthening the relationship without getting mired in adolescent battles.

Theresa Decker, *marriage and family therapist*

After years of working with parents of tweens and teens Tish understands the challenges parents face and what our kids really need. Refreshing in its no-nonsense advice and wisdom, this is the perfect book for parents of tweens and teens to keep by their bedside table or to read first thing in the morning as a reminder of what really matters and how to love their kids well.

Sheryl Gould, *founder of Moms of Tweens and Teens, speaker and author*

Parents all want the same thing: a lifelong relationship with their children. Fear of losing that bond or making fatal relational mistakes makes some parents try to be more of a friend than a life-guide for their children. Tish offers one hundred ideas to help parents preserve the loving connection through the push-and-pull years of adolescence. She includes smart ways to implement modern technology without diminishing the gift of old-fashioned wisdom that can be sent across a generational bridge teens can easily embrace.

Gail Goolsby, *MA, MEd, ACC, counselor, life coach*

Love your children, and let them know you love them. Children who experience love find it far easier to believe God loves them.

BILLY GRAHAM

Copyright © 2018 by Letitia Suk

Cover and interior design by Jeff Jansen | www.AestheticSoup.net. Cover art: Creative Market: DOT DASH | Seamless Patterns by Jenna Maxfield. Cover copyright © 2018 by Hachette Book Group, Inc.

Hachette Book Group supports the right to free expression and the value of copyright. The purpose of copyright is to encourage writers and artists to produce the creative works that enrich our culture.

The scanning, uploading, and distribution of this book without permission is a theft of the author's intellectual property. If you would like permission to use material from the book (other than for review purposes), please contact permissions@hbgusa.com. Thank you for your support of the author's rights.

Ellie Claire
Hachette Book Group
1290 Avenue of the Americas, New York, NY 10104
ellieclaire.com

First Edition: February 2019

Ellie Claire is a division of Hachette Book Group, Inc. The Ellie Claire name and logo are trademarks of Hachette Book Group, Inc.

The publisher is not responsible for websites (or their content) that are not owned by the publisher.

Scripture references marked NIV are from the Holy Bible, New International Version®, NIV®. Copyright © 1973, 1978, 1984, 2011 by Biblica, Inc.® All rights reserved worldwide. | Scripture quotations marked MSG are from *The Message*. Copyright © 1993, 1994, 1995, 1996, 2000, 2001, 2002 by Eugene H. Peterson. Used by permission of NavPress Publishing Group. | Scripture quotations marked NLT are taken from the Holy Bible, New Living Translation, copyright © 1996, 2004, 2007 by Tyndale House Foundation. Used by permission of Tyndale House Publishers, Inc., Carol Stream, Illinois 60188. All rights reserved. | Scripture quotations marked NKJV are taken from the New King James Version®. Copyright © 1982 by Thomas Nelson. Used by permission. All rights reserved.

Library of Congress Cataloging-in-Publication Data has been applied for.

ISBN: 978-1-63326-209-6 (hardcover)

Printed in China

RRD

10 9 8 7 6 5 4 3 2 1

Introduction

Books, blog posts, and podcasts abound
on how to parent teens, but today's busy
mom doesn't have time to get to them.
*100 Need-to-Know Tips for Moms of Tweens
and Teens* is a grab-and-go guide to read
along the way. Each short, stand-alone
tip provides an immediate opportunity to
strengthen your relationship with your teen.

A primary task of parenting teens is to establish
a bond of closeness that can be drawn on for the
long journey ahead. This book focuses on forming
the adult–adult relationship that will outlast these
exciting, fun-filled, and often challenging years.

Looking for help? Reaching for hope? You will
find it here. In the end, it's not the right rules,
but the right relationship that lasts a lifetime.

1

Leave on a Positive Note

When your teen leaves the house for an outing with friends, make a point to say, "Goodbye, have a good time! You look great. I love you." The last few moments of your interaction can set the tone for the rest of the evening for both of you. If your teen leaves the house feeling good about you and about themselves, they will carry those positive feelings with them. Likewise, if they leave home feeling angry, misunderstood, or belittled, those negative feelings will accompany them. If you really want to make an impression, give them a hug and occasionally slip them a little unasked-for cash.

Remember, the best deterrent to risky teen behavior is a good parental relationship.

2

Keep Texts Friendly

Chances are, your teen prefers texting over most other forms of communication. Choosing to use this tool in a friendly way is a great way to stay in touch. Tell them you love them and are praying for their test. Ask them if they need anything from Target or send fun tidbits of information. You can text questions like, "When will the car be back?" "Will you be home for dinner?" "Could you please pick up a gallon of milk?"

Decide that you will only use this creative tool for positive thoughts or simple questions. This is not the vehicle to complain ("the kitchen is a wreck"), criticize ("you never leave gas in the car"), or accuse ("you were out too late last night"). Keep it upbeat, and they'll keep opening your texts. Don't, and they'll soon ignore them.

3

Ask, Don't Tell

*J*ust like you, your teen will respond far more positively when *asked* to do something rather than *told* to do it. Consider the difference in tone between these examples: "Could you pick up your sister for me?" as opposed to "Go pick up your sister. Now." This works the same for household help. "Could you give me a hand with clearing the table?" instead of, "Don't leave the house without helping with dinner cleanup."

Treat your teen with respect, kindness, and flexibility. Wording requests respectfully, such as "Sometime this evening, would you . . ." rather than "Do it now," will help build an overall family atmosphere of cooperation and appreciation. While you're at it, be sure to say *please* and *thank you* and watch to see how those gestures will come back to you.

4

Respond with Enthusiasm

....

Does the new-idea component of your teen's brain seem to be stuck on automatic pilot? A fresh thought pops out every few hours: "I'm going to start a rock band." "I want to dye my hair blue." "I'm thinking about taking a road trip after high school." You get the gist.

Years of experience has taught me that the best response (unless the idea violates your ethical or moral values) is enthusiasm: "That would be fun" or "What an interesting possibility" or "Tell me more." When your teen has freedom to daydream out loud, they will usually come to wise choices. When every off-beat idea is shot down or ridiculed, they can feel undermined, judged, or misunderstood—and that can drive them to make the whim a reality. When at a loss for words, try "Wow!"

5

Ask Permission before Giving Advice

You've been around the block many times since your own teenage years, and it's easy to be ready with advice from that experience. As tempting as it is to jump in with your take on their situation, however, try asking for permission first. Ask, "I have a couple thoughts on this; can I share them?"

Gaining their permission doesn't just get their attention; it opens up a better chance that they will listen. The brief pause also gives you a moment to gather that nugget of wisdom. Of course, they might say no—if they do, save the advice for a better opportunity. When they are more receptive, it will come.

What do girls do
who haven't any mothers
to help them through
their troubles?

LOUISA MAY ALCOTT

6

Rewind That Conversation

I'm sure you've found yourself in more than one rushed, heated, confrontational, or "bad attitude" conversation with your teen. Whether the attitude is coming from you or directed toward you, a simple way to change the tone is to ask for a do-over.

"Do you think we could start this conversation over?" is a good question before the escalation rises off the charts. "Let's try this again" also works. When emotion is high, a simple, "Whoa, let's start over, please," is an effective phrase. A rewind allows time to move the conversation in a more positive direction.

7

Plan a Road Trip

The quintessential road-trip refrain, "Are we there yet?" has now often been replaced with silence as your teen listens to music, texts their friends, surfs social media, or sleeps. Don't take it personally. Give your teen some ownership in the venture by asking their opinion about restaurant choices, activities for the day, and even departure times. If your teen is licensed, you can ensure their focus by asking them to help drive.

Offering choices works well too. "Who wants to go to a water park or rock climbing, and who wants to hang by the pool or go shopping?" Each family member chooses their activity for the day, and everyone comes back together for an evening meal or activity. Respect the need for downtime amid a lot of family togetherness. You'll all benefit from that.

*Point your kids
in the right direction —
when they're old
they won't be lost.*

PROVERBS 22:6 MSG

8

Schedule Some Fun at the End of Summer

*B*efore your teen goes back to school, use one of the waning days of summer for a date. Plan something you know they want to do. Ask them what that would be.

Rather than inviting them in person, try a text, private message, or note on their bed along the lines of "Hey, let's hang out before you go back to school. Ideas?" It's a good way to start the ball rolling.

Another approach is to make a list of ideas, including some sure wins like eating and shopping, and ask your teen (by text, email, or conversation) to choose a couple things that look like fun. Plan your outing as soon as possible after the invite.

9

Remember: This Too Shall Pass

Remember the terrible twos? That picky child who would eat nothing but chicken nuggets and Fruit Roll-Ups? The one who refused to potty-train? These are the pressing dilemmas of moms of young kids, but wouldn't you sometimes like to trade your current issues with your teen for those early ones? But like those early bumps in the road, the sticky points of today will also eventually be resolved. I remember receiving a spiritual nudge in the middle of a particular teen crisis, the idea that I was only in the middle of the book, so to speak. The plot was not yet resolved, so I should keep reading. In other words, Mom, encourage yourself: it ain't over yet—no matter what's pushing your buttons right now, that too shall pass!

10

"Welcome Home!"

Greetings are important. Business deals and political maneuvers are shaped by the cultural norms for the greeting. Bowing, hand shaking, air-kissing, hugging . . . they all work in different contexts. As your first contact with your teen after school, set the stage for whatever comes next with a warm greeting.

Work on eye contact, a touch, or a hug; set aside your own agenda for the few minutes it will take to let your teen know you're glad to see them. Save any leftover issues from the morning or day before for a later time. If you start with the towels on the floor as soon as you see them, you might lose them for the rest of the night. Your teen probably has many choices of where to stop after school. You want them to be glad they came home!

Home is the place we should
return to with eager spirits,
the journey's end we reach
with sighs of contentment.

KAREN BURTON MAINS

11

Sit Down to Dinner

*I*f your dinner menu includes frozen pizza, Chinese takeout, or bowls of cereal, you're not alone. Somewhere back in the 1980s or '90s, family dinners began to include TVs and fast food. The "family" part of the description often simply meant you were all eating in the car together on the way to another soccer game.

Reviving the sit-down-at-the-table-and-talk dinner as many evenings as possible is an excellent way to stay in touch with your teen. Consider the meal a family bonding opportunity, not just a time to eat. Setting the table long before dinner is ready announces that this is an event, even if it is just dinner on a Tuesday night. Posting menus for the week on the side of the fridge can work wonders for attendance when favorite meals are included.

12

Put Your Teen in the Driver's Seat

Is your teen getting their driver's permit soon? Look at this as a great opportunity to spend time together, bonding in the car. When *you* drive, they can tune you out, stay glued to their phone, or sleep. When *they* drive, they have to interact with you.

Many states require at least twenty-five hours of supervised driving before a permit can be issued. That's twenty-five hours of hangout time you wouldn't have otherwise had. Once they have that license, it might be days or even weeks before you're in a car together again!

When there is an opportunity to travel in the same car, ask your teen to drive. More conversation will happen when they're in the driver's seat.

Presence is more than just being there.

MALCOLM FORBES

13

Use the Power of the Positive Spin

. . . .

Spinning isn't just for merry-go-rounds or exercise classes. Reporters, Realtors, and perpetually optimistic individuals know the power of reframing something negative through a positive perspective. Putting that spin to work in the way we talk to our teens is just as powerful.

When you muse, *This kid is never home*, text or message, "I miss you when you're not here." When you want to scream, *Do you think you could lift a finger to help me*, say instead, "I really appreciate it when you pitch in around here." Though you're terrified at the thought of them getting a driver's license, casually remark, "I know you'll be a great driver." Look for the positive spin; it's not that hard to find. Positive thinking not only encourages them; it can change your outlook too.

14
Get Online

I remember a three-day argument with my daughter, during which we spoke not a single word to each other. We did, however, email each other our positions on a situation that we needed to resolve. Over the course of the interaction, we each compromised and landed at a good place. I don't even remember what it was about, but I do remember that the technique worked.

Today, texting, private messaging, or social media sharing is a great way to remind your teen about dates they need to keep track of, upcoming deadlines, or family outings. Sometimes a situation is too emotionally charged for an immediate face-to-face, and a text can be a safer way to wade into a discussion.

Nothing beats being present with your teen when it's time for a heart-to-heart talk, but online communication can open a new level of your relationship.

15

Be Involved at Your Teen's School

Do you know who's who and what's what at your teen's school? Many parents who were quite involved at the elementary school level become PTA dropouts by the time their child hits high school. How can you be invested without being overbearing?

- Go to parent-teacher conferences. Ask about course work, direction for the class, and how you can help.

- Most teachers provide email addresses. Drop them an occasional note of thanks.

- Attend sports, music, and other events. You won't regret it later.

- If you suspect your teen is falling behind at school or needs special testing, find out and pursue a resolution.

Nothing is more important than the parent learning how to effectively meet the teen's emotional need for love.

GARY CHAPMAN

16

Ask for Your Teen's Opinion and Advice

....

A great way to connect with your teen is to ask their opinion about something in your life: "Should I wear black or brown shoes with this?" "I'm thinking about switching our ISP. What do you know about ___?" "Could you take a look at these decorating ideas and tell me which you think would work best?" or "What's a good movie to watch tonight?"

To move deeper, ask their advice: "I'm thinking about going part-time; do you have any thoughts on that?" "Grandma seems to be slipping a bit. Any ideas on how I can help her?" or "My friend seems to be pulling back a bit. Has that ever happened to you?"

Connecting with your teen by asking their opinions and advice taps in to different aspects of your relationship and can be beneficial for both of you.

17

Agree to Disagree

Yankees or Cubs, vegetarian or paleo, republican or democrat—opinions and preferences vary widely within a family. Some of these opposing views make for friendly teasing, while others are closer to the heart. Part of the task of adolescence is learning to be separate from the parent, and that can include choosing the opposite side of a parent's position on anything. This is normal.

Teens are learning to think critically; they're trying on different opinions and sorting out what they really believe—and they practice on you! A lot of what looks like a decision is really a step in the process. So get used to rooting for opposing teams, enjoying different dinner entrees, and even canceling out each other's votes in elections. Give your teen room to think out loud. Choosing to agree to disagree now will result in a closer relationship later.

*Adolescence is not
about letting go.
It's about hanging on
during a very bumpy ride.*

RON TAFFEL

18

Try Some Bedtime Strategies

Teens need a lot of sleep with all that brain development going on, but how can we help shape their sleep habits when we often go to bed before they do? Here are a few ideas.

- Establish a bedtime to ensure about nine hours of sleep a night. It won't always work, but persist in your goal, especially with younger teens.

- Ask for a homework time estimate, so bedtime isn't compromised more than on occasion.

- Put phones and computers to bed too. Designate a place for the phone overnight.

- Start turning off lights and quieting the house about thirty minutes before bed.

- Intentionally say goodnight to your teen with a hug, a kiss, or a prayer.

19

Be the Expert

....

Experts on teens, even in faith communities, take different sides on lots of topics. Homework, curfews, entertainment choices . . . to name a few. Each one's opinion can seem so right.

One expert's advice will work wonders on one teen and fall flat on another. Some advice may be consistent with your value system; some will be directly opposed. As the parent, you are the expert on your kid. You generally know what will be effective and what won't. Find the fit for your family. If one specialist's technique doesn't appeal to you, keep looking. Like with shoes, while the style can be attractive, it's the fit that counts.

20

Support the Extracurriculars

"A child needs to find a niche, or a niche will find them," a wise teacher once told us. This is especially relevant for parents of teens. While parents are rightfully concerned about extreme time commitments, extracurriculars can keep kids busy, focused, and often too tired for much mischief. In our family, sports were important, and grades were often the best during the active season as our teens learned to study more efficiently between practices. The same can be said of music, theater, debate, dance, or whatever attracts your teen.

Feeding their interest by following through with lessons, encouraging tryouts, and attending events helps your teen take ownership of their niche and shape their sense of self around something positive. As an added perk, you might enjoy the relationships you make with other parents who are also involved.

A family should be a place where comfort is experienced and understood, so that the people are prepared to give comfort to others.

EDITH SCHAEFFER

21

Encourage Extended Family Relationships

....

*I*n describing a visit with his grandparents, my seventeen-year-old son remarked, "I enjoy it less but appreciate it more than I did when I was younger." Whether your family's extended relationships are wonderful or crazy, families are priceless. Teens, however, can lose sight of that truth in all the drama of their lives. Do your best to keep them involved. Remember, they've begun making their own plans and they may have work or other obligations, so give them plenty of notice of family events, especially around the holidays.

If you see extended family often, save the you-need-to-be-there stance for important occasions. If such gatherings are infrequent events, help your teen to treasure them, even if they don't yet understand why. The memories your teen makes now may well shape their future role as a grandparent.

22

Know When to Seek Help

There may come a time when the situation you are in with your teen requires some additional assistance. Don't worry—help is available, and many parents utilize these resources. Trained clergy, therapists, school counselors, and medical providers can be part of your team and will know what to look for. How do you know when to make the call?

- Your teen seems to have lost interest in engaging in life.

- You suspect drug or alcohol abuse.

- You see signs of self-harm.

- Your teen (or a friend) comes to you, asking for help.

- Your teen's grades slip suddenly and unexpectedly.

- Your teen has dropped their old friends for new ones you don't trust.

*T*here's no way
to be a perfect mother
and a million ways
to be a good one.

JILL CHURCHILL

23

Avoid Micromanaging Your Teen's Faith

It's been said that God has no grandchildren—which simply means we must each have our own faith experience, separate from that of our parents. In our spiritually aware culture, most teens are searching for something/someone to believe in. Your teen's faith journey might parallel yours, lag behind, or leap ahead. It's quite likely that your faith experience differed from that of your parents; in the same way, don't expect your teen's experience to mirror yours.

Your role as a parent is to provide spiritual training but not to force their faith development. Nurture your teen's faith through your prayers, your example, and your encouragement, but trust God to work out the big picture. Keep in mind, His timing is rarely the same as ours.

24

Don't Play Twenty Questions

Who wants to play twenty questions? Not your teen! One of the most common gripes teens make about parents is that they ask too many questions. Face it, we usually want to know more data than what we're given, so the barrage of questions begins.

To keep the conversation going without the twenty questions, try the well-known therapist technique of listening to your teen, responding with "*hmm . . . oh . . . okay.*" Let them talk while you nod a bit and perhaps interject a "wow," "really," or "interesting" often enough to keep them talking. What feels like the FBI to them is often just conversation to us. You'll get more information this way than by continuing the game no one wants to play.

25

Listen to Their Passion

....

When I see teens marching and holding signs, I'm reminded of my own participation in rallies and get-out-the-vote campaigns . . . and how much I wanted my parents to understand and support my involvement.

Your teen likely feels strongly about many issues, including hot topics like racism, gun control, and free speech, to name a few. Regardless of whether you agree with their stance, hear them out. Be their audience; engage in debate. You'll probably learn some new things too.

When you listen to their passion, you validate their voice. They will need that the rest of their lives.

Parents, don't come down too hard on your children or you'll crush their spirits.

COLOSSIANS 3:21 MSG

26

Take a Deep Breath, Say a Prayer, and Wait

....

When your teen presents you with troubling information, your most effective parenting technique may be to wait. Take a deep breath, say a quick prayer, and just wait. Often your teen will feel uncomfortable with the silence and talk more.

While an immediate response is occasionally required, most of us could use some space—and it's okay to say that: "Wow, I need to do some processing here" or "I'd like to think about this a little while and get back to you." Usually it's best not to engage when you can't see where you're headed, and the waiting will bring perspective. Take the initiative—set a time when you will discuss the situation, whether after dinner, tomorrow morning, or whenever. The wait is usually worth it.

27

Take a Mom Moment

....

Despite our efforts to listen well, speak slowly, and wait to respond, sometimes a lecture is just waiting to happen. When I really want to say something that sounds like a lecture, I call it that. I say, "I need to have a Mom moment here!"

"Mom moments" might sound like this: "Don't *ever* get in a car when the driver has been drinking!" or "There are some movies no one should ever see!" or "What are those girls thinking, wearing those clothes?" Whatever the theme, speak your mind, elaborate on the topic, and be honest but respectful, just as you would expect them to be. Afterward, say, "Mom moment over; thanks for listening," and resume normal activity. It's an effective tool when used with care.

Affirmations for
your teenagers
are absolutely a must.

ANNE ORTLUND

28

Praise Your Teen in Public

....

Too often, parents criticize or complain about their teens instead of presenting them well. When you get the chance to talk about your teen with your coworkers, acquaintances, or even relatives, start with something good. Try, "Let me brag about my girl/guy a minute."

Sure, there's security and relief in camaraderie—i.e., our teens drive us crazy, and we all know it—but there is something startling and refreshing about a mom who openly expresses her affection and appreciation for her teen. Be *that* mom.

29

Find the Connection

....

Most strong relationships start with a solid connecting point. Maybe you read the same authors, vote similarly, share faith journeys, or enjoy the same TV show. To build a strong relationship with your teen, find what connects you outside the parental relationship itself. What extra bonds do you share with your teen? A penchant for Thai food? A love of British films? Thrifting? College basketball? Reality TV shows? Trying new recipes?

Even if your interest is less than theirs, revving up any common, pleasant link will feed the connection between you and your teen. Some days, that connection will be your strongest link.

30

Look for the Best

....

A common complaint from parents of teens is that outside of the home, their teen is compassionate, sensitive, and quick to help others, while at home they can be silent, sullen, or sarcastic. The famous biblical passage on love describes many attributes, including that love "always looks for the best" (1 Corinthians 13:7 MSG).

For parents of teens, that means just that—identify the best part of your teen and feed it with your admiration and appreciation. It may still take a while for those other attributes to show up at home, but showing love by believing they are there is a place to start.

*Live in the moment
and make it so beautiful
that it will be worth remembering.*

IDA SCOTT TAYLOR MCKINNEY

31

Make a Big Deal Out of the Launch

Since Day 1, letting them go has been on your parenting agenda, even if you ignored it. Good thing you've got all senior year to prepare, because, ready or not, here it comes.

How can you make the last summer after high school memorable and send them off with a bang?

- Display confidence all summer that they will succeed.

- Let this be their moment—focus on the start of their adventure, not on you falling apart.

- Involve them in planning a special party or dinner to celebrate.

- Create a special send-off ritual or gift, such as giving a blessing, writing them a letter, or presenting a collection of photos.

32

Love Me, Love My Friends

I recently attended a birthday party for a friend where most of the guests were midlife women (like me!) who didn't know each other. My friend was so excited for all of us to meet each other and hoped we would connect well. It was a fun evening. In much the same way, your teen wants you to like their friends, the people they have chosen to share this segment of their life's journey.

Treat their friends as you would your own friends, with respect, politeness, laughter, and welcome. Learn their birthdays, favorite snacks, and the classes they are taking. Greet them by name and offer food often. You will build your relationship with your teen by connecting with their friends.

Each day of our lives
we make deposits
in the memory banks
of our children.

CHARLES R. SWINDOLL

33

Be That Home

....

You likely remember which of your high school friends' homes you felt most welcome in. It probably wasn't the best decorated or even the best-kept house on the block. But it was the place where you were warmly greeted, fed well—even if just with popcorn and water—and spoken to as a real person.

Now it's your chance to offer that great hangout place for your teen's friends. Prepare for the invasions with stashes of pop, pizza, cookies, chips, and healthier options. Be around, but not too obvious. Your social life might need to adjust for a few years to be available, but it could mean some of the best fun you've ever had!

34

Bless the Friends You Don't Like

*I*t's true—you won't like all your teen's friends. Unfortunately, announcing your dislike can quickly elevate that person to sainthood in your teen's mind. Be careful about this unless your teen is in danger or at serious risk from a friend.

Instead find something positive to say about the friend: "I like the way ____ is [passionate about causes] [knows a lot about music] [isn't afraid to be different]." Then you can casually say something like, "I *am* a little concerned about his/her [driving] [lying] [poor relationship with parents]." Follow with, "What do you think about that?" Then listen and don't comment. Wait to see if your impression was wrong or if your teen recognizes the drawbacks of this relationship.

35

Give Enough Notice

. . . .

You know the experience of being interrupted after sitting down to eat, settling down to watch TV, or snuggling up to read a book. That unwanted phone call, unexpected house repair, or unavoidable errand can be so irritating.

That's what it's like for a teen when we interrupt their activity to tell them to set the table or pick up their sister or that you need them to babysit the younger kids tonight. These are reasonable requests, but giving a little notice can make a big difference in how they're received. Try a more considerate approach: "When you're done with that game, please take the garbage out." "I know it's an hour from now, but would you pick up your sister for me at five?" "We need someone to watch the kids this weekend. Would that work for you?" Keep the light tone as you work out the details.

*Pray that your children
will develop hearts
that seek after God.*

STORMIE OMARTIAN

36

Stick with "I" Statements

If you've ever read a self-help book or article on relationships, you know this is a biggie. Using "I" statements about your feelings rather than "you" comments about their actions can go a long way to diffusing a situation.

For example, "I feel disregarded when you get out of the car without saying goodbye or thanks" is much less confrontational than, "You never say thanks." Similarly, "I feel hurt when you raise your voice at me" is better than "You're always yelling at me." Think about what you feel, then try to get it into one word you can use to express that emotion. Instead of pulling you into a fight, diplomacy might get you out of one.

37

Use Specific Affirmations

....

While any positive comment toward your teen counts, the more specific you can be, the better. "You are so responsible" is nice, but "I like the way I can count on you to call when your plans change" is better. Likewise, while "You are so smart" is good, "You really worked hard on that English paper, and it payed off" says more.

Think about what you've noticed or want to build up in your teen, then be as specific as possible in expressing your appreciation of it. It also helps both of you to know that while they're not always "so reliable," they can be counted on to remember to pick up the milk!

Speak a word
of affirmation at
the right moment
in a child's life,
and it's like lighting up
a whole roomful
of possibilities.

GARY SMALLEY

38

Be Proud

....

$\mathcal{R}$eese Witherspoon's comments to her parents at the 2006 Oscars made a deep impression on me. "I'm so blessed to have my family here tonight," she said. "My mother and my father are here. And I just want to say thank you so much for everything, for being so proud of me. It didn't matter if I was making my bed or makin' a movie. They never hesitated to say how proud they were of me, and that means so very much to a child. So, thank you, Mom and Dad."

Your teen might not win an Academy Award, but their need for your affirmation, whether for making the bed or making a movie, for playing their flute or running the bases, for picking up the milk or dropping off their sister, is just as critical.

And someday, they might just tell the world how important that was.

39

Avoid the Bait and Switch.

....

Inviting your teen out for a fun activity usually ensures their presence, but don't use that activity as a gateway to bring up an issue or push an agenda they're not willing to approach. If they expect to hang out and you get them there and give them a lecture instead, they're likely to shut you out. Furthermore, your trustworthy score has just taken a big hit.

While you're out having fun, look for the opportunity to plan the next date. Each date with your teen is a part of cementing your long-term relationship for the years ahead. You'll have more opportunity to get to the big issues and tough conversations when you've established a strong relationship of trust through fun.

40

Try Cooperation over Coercion

I once hung a sign over my kitchen sink that said, "No dishes in here." My husband later took a picture of it . . . posted above a sink full of dishes! I clearly needed to find another tactic. Dishes in the sink, towels on the floor, an unkempt car: these are often points of conflict. Coercing a teen might work if the reward is sweet enough or the consequences bitter enough, but the prize-winning formula is cooperation, not coercion.

Start with, "You might not even notice, but it really bugs me when _____. I could yell and scream, but what do you think would work?" Teens will often surprise you with their wisdom when asked to help solve a stalemate. If at all possible, try their plan. When they are a part of the solution, there's usually less of a problem.

*T*hose who wait on the L**ORD**
shall renew their strength;
they shall mount up with wings
like eagles, they shall run
and not be weary,
they shall walk and not faint.

ISAIAH 40:31 NKJV

41

Play at a Play

....

When brainstorming for ideas for parent-teen hangouts, consider attending a live theater performance. From Shakespeare to *Les Mis*, a play is a common winner with both daughters and sons.

A play is distinct enough from a movie to be special. It can be saved for, planned for, and looked forward to long in advance. Most metro areas have a variety of options to choose from, especially in the summer with outdoor performances. Half-price tickets may be available for day-of performances for the spontaneous mom, while popular, pricier performances may offer lotteries.

What may seem like an extravagant cost will pay off in lifetime memories. To further preserve the experience, get the soundtrack and play it often.

42

Teach Your Kids to Honor Dad

....

I knew a mom whose husband walked out when the kids were young. Yet she told me her number-one goal was for them to have a good relationship with him. She realized things were going to be harder for the kids after the divorce and knew a poor relationship with their dad would only make things worse. To that end, she vowed to herself never to speak negatively about him to the kids. When I checked in with her years later, those kids had a close relationship with their dad, and she had no regrets about encouraging that.

Help your teen to honor their dad by your words and example. Let them hear and see your appreciation and affirmation. You have a big role to play now in shaping their lifetime relationship for the future.

*C*hildren are our
second chance
to have a great
parent-child relationship.

LAURA SCHLESSINGER

43

Respect Their Privacy

A wise mom once said that the teenage years can be compared to a butterfly in a cocoon. It is best not to pick at the cocoon but to protect it so that at the end, the strong young adult can emerge. One of the ways we pick at our kids' cocoons is by not respecting their privacy.

Most teens are not involved in covert behavior behind closed doors. Mostly they are creating physical and emotional space from you—the same way you did years ago, when you locked yourself in the bathroom for some alone time! Knock on the door before you enter; stay out of their room when they're not home; and don't read that journal! Life-or-death issues like drug use, illegal activity, or significant depression are exceptions, but good boundaries make beautiful butterflies.

44

Celebrate Independence

One thing I love about the Fourth of July is that everyone celebrates it! Like Thanksgiving, it is a holiday the whole culture is a part of. Barbecues, parades, and fireworks unite us all for a day.

Your teens are developing their own declarations of independence. This is, after all, their primary task . . . to separate from us in a healthy way. Like most transitions, this is not always smooth. They're often ready for much more independence than we're ready to give, and accepting that is all part of the process. When your teen seems to be breaking away, remember that it's normal and appropriate. You did the same with your parents. Your assignment is to let go gradually and gracefully, finishing the task you started the day they were born.

45

Break Out the Takeout

*I*f you're in a season that feels like each family member is in a different orbit, try using a fun dinner to get aligned. Notes on the bathroom mirror announcing, "Chinese takeout tonight, what do you want?" can result in perfect attendance at the table.

Sending a text around asking what kind of pizza everyone would like is another effective tactic. Or you could try offering ice cream sundaes with several flavors and toppings or root beer floats on a hot summer night. If you are stuck for ideas, ask them what sounds good. When I tried that, I ended up cooking a turkey with stuffing in July, but it was a hit, and the payoff was getting our orbits aligned, at least for an evening!

Mother love is the fuel that enables a normal human being to do the impossible.

MARION C. GARRETTY

46

Chill, Mom!

You often don't see it coming. What seems like an easy conversation, friendly warning, or a little reminder blows up. All of a sudden, two words spew from your darling teen's lips, "Chill, Mom!" Somewhere in the interchange you crossed a line you didn't see! Concern is heard as freaking out; a simple request lands as nagging; a request for clarification comes across as inquisition. What is the best response? Usually to chill, Mom!

Backing off with an "Okay, honey" or a "Sorry, just being a mom here; got carried away" or a "You're right, let's talk about this later" is often the best response. Regardless of your best intentions, a momentary wall has gone up, and attempts to keep talking will just make it worse. Taking the request to chill now usually warms things up again later.

47

Make a Homework Deal

Have you ever known a teen who loved being bugged about homework? Yeah, me neither. Instead, try making a deal: "I think we both want you to do well in school, right? Let's see if that can happen without me being the homework police." (Cheers!) Ask them how you can be assured that they've got it under control. Don't settle for a "Don't worry about it." Stay calm but firm in that you just want to know what the plan is.

Decide together which activities are okay on school nights. Ask about their strategies for study. Agree on policies for social media during the homework block. Once a plan is in motion, be careful not to reinstate nagging. If the plan is not getting results, talk to your teen about setting up a new plan. Be focused on the plan, not on them.

It is not until you become a mother that your judgment slowly turns to compassion and understanding.

ERMA BOMBECK

48

Watch Out for Trustbusters

I once read a note I found on the floor of my thirteen-year-old's room. It wasn't written to me, but I freely commented on it to my teen. That was a serious mistake. The incident was recently brought up again, many years after the fact, but I think I've now finally apologized enough. Trustbusters work both ways—we expect our teens to earn our trust, but as moms, we have to watch our own trust lines in building healthy lifetime relationships with our teens.

Common trustbusters include snooping around their rooms *just in case* there might be something interesting to find, peeking at their texts out of curiosity, and intentionally eavesdropping on conversations behind closed doors. When in doubt about whether a search warrant is justified (and sometimes it is), ask yourself how you would feel if you got caught snooping or what you would do if they started reading your journal.

49

Keep Accounts Short

....

Driving my son to college for his first year opened the confessional. Worried that there might be unfinished business between us that would get in the way of his view of me in the days ahead, I plunged in with all my regrets. "Remember when I made you walk when you missed the bus? I should have given you a ride"; "I wish I had gone to more of your games"; and so on. He mostly said, "That's okay, Mom," but it really felt good to clear my heart.

I try to remember now to keep short accounts. "I really wasn't listening when you were telling me about school. Can you try again?" "I was quick to judge, but I realize I was wrong."

You might not get an immediate, heartfelt response, but trust that you were heard and let that minimize the regret buildup.

50

Bring Back Tea Parties

Many health benefits are ascribed to drinking tea, as are relational benefits too. Tea parties aren't just for the little ones. Many varieties of tea are available, and a tea excursion is fun. Don't forget the props like teapots, cozies, strainers for loose tea, and delicious treats like scones, muffins, or special cookies just for these occasions.

Prepare a tray with tea, mugs, and treats, then invite your teen to join you. If you sense a bit of resistance, show up at their door with the tray for a study break. Tea is a slow drink and a great way to connect. Teatime is not the place for a talk about your agenda; it should be a shared downtime in a busy day. It can also be a great after-school or evening ritual and could even replace milk and cookies for comfort food.

*Your success as a family . . .
our success as a society . . .
depends not on what happens
at the White House, but on what
happens inside your house.*

BARBARA BUSH

51

Get Good at Reading Your Teen

My husband was always amazed when I warned him, "When you say this, she's going to say that." I had figured out which teen was easily offended, which one didn't even hear the first request, and which one loved to argue just for the fun of it.

Knowing how to read your teen is a skill that serves both parent and teen well. Are they more cooperative after school or after dinner? How does exhaustion or hunger affect your teen? Is there a correlation between their outburst and an incident at school? If they love to debate, how much bantering needs to occur before you can get down to the real issue?

Reading your teen helps you to know when to bring up a topic and when to let it rest. Give it a try—it's never too late to start observing.

52

It's Not Your Fault!

....

*W*ell, not all of it! In our family, there was a joke that no matter what happens to any of the kids, even the faraway ones, it was Mom's fault. We can all laugh, but for many moms, that feels too close to the truth. Many of our teen's choices are just that: our *teen's* choices. Hormones, brain development, personality types, learning styles, birth order—these are just a few of the components that influence them at any given time. Teens are in the continual process of growing up, and much of that process is trial and error. Their trial; their error.

As someone once pointed out, God was a perfect parent and His kids (Adam and Eve) still blew it. Piling guilt on yourself—*it's all my fault*—takes power away from both of you.

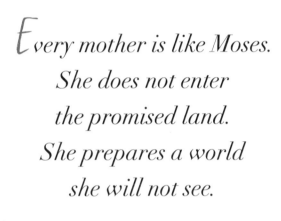

*Every mother is like Moses.
She does not enter
the promised land.
She prepares a world
she will not see.*

POPE PAUL VI

53

Engage Politically

....

A pending election is an opportunity to listen to what your teen is thinking about current issues and direction. Try this script:

You: "What do you think about the governor's race this year?"

Them: "Whatever."

You: "I don't know that much, either. I do think they differ on _____. Do you have an opinion on that?"

Them: [Hopefully, a comment.]

You: "Good point. Any other thoughts?"

Them: [Other thoughts.]

You: "I appreciate hearing what you're thinking."

TV ads can start conversation too. Whether you're on different sides of the issues or equally in the dark, connecting in conversation is always a winner.

54

Create a Fun Food Tradition

Saturday pizza night is a long-standing tradition in our household. "Who's coming for pizza" was the standard question each week. When the kids were little, we served it picnic-style on the floor. Later, their friends got in on the fun, creating many varieties, like spinach and feta, barbecue chicken, pesto, and veggie. Whatever the week's specialty, it always drew a crowd to our kitchen.

This idea can work just as well on any weeknight and with any fun cuisine. The continuity of the same menu each week (though plain chicken probably wouldn't have the same effect) creates a "this is how we do it in our family" identity. Teens need tradition, even when it seems like they are pushing us away. If the reviews are good, repeat it in a week. Soon it will be a family bond.

55

Put on
Your Nurse's Cap

....

From colds, flu, mono, wisdom teeth removal, and more, your teen will at some point be home sick. These ailments can be a great opportunity to provide loads of TLC. If you can, use one of your own sick days to stay home with them.

- Download and watch some favorite old movies or TV shows together.
- Start a Monopoly game.
- Offer a back rub.
- Deliver a tea and toast tray.
- Break out the cards for Crazy Eights.

A few extra doses of mom love can provide immunity to lots of other teen ailments!

If you want your children to turn out well, spend twice as much time with them, and half as much money.

ABIGAIL VAN BUREN

56

Start Talking about New Year's Eve Early

....

As adults, we sometimes feel that New Year's Eve is a bit overrated, but to most teens, the night is full of magic and possibility. For that reason, the time to start talking about it is way before, not the day before. Careful conversation and planning can make a huge difference in both of your expectations for the evening.

Be upbeat, positive, but firm in your guidelines. "A party sounds great; which parents will be there?" Call the parents to confirm. "I'm not expecting you to drink, but others might. Can you say no?" "Sure, your friends can come over; we'll be home. What kind of snacks would you like?" Take a nap so you can stay awake later. Remind them to give you a call if they want to leave early or need a ride—no questions asked. It works to build trust both ways.

57

Take in the Long View

*I*n the midst of a long stream of busy days and full weekends, it's important to remember the long view. What do you need to impart to your teen? What do you want them to remember? Are you investing in a lifetime relationship with them? Will what just happened be remembered in ten years? (Probably not, but how you responded to it might.)

Remembering the long view can keep you focused on building your relationship and catching yourself when you're tearing it down. It can help you "be quick to listen, slow to speak, and slow to get angry" (James 1:19 NLT). We've shared lots of laughs over the dumb things I have said and done over the years, but the long-view perspective usually is the best.

*The child that never learns
to obey his parents
in the home will not
obey God or man
out of the home.*

SUSANNA WESLEY

58

Protect Their Ears for the Future

TV shows seem quieter these days as I need to "go up a few notches" in the volume on a regular basis. Or maybe it's the result of all the music I blasted back in my day.

Specialists agree that if the music can be heard from the headphones three feet away, it is in the unsafe range. Consider instating a three-foot policy in your home; use a yardstick to make it fun. As an experiment, ask your teen to put cotton balls or earplugs in their ears for an entire evening, to replicate mild hearing loss. If that fails, how about, "Turn it down or turn it off; your choice!"

59

Accept the Music

....

Most teens know who's hot and who's not in the music scene. In their earbuds or through the speakers, music is the soundtrack of their lives. We sometimes want to turn it down, turn it off, or tune it out, but we know it's not going away. Every generation of parents has had issues with their kids' music. The question is, how will you respond? Here are some positive ideas:

- Listen to it with your teen.

- Ask them what they like about the music and what it says to them.

- Express your concerns about the lyrics, but don't lecture. Converse.

- Avoid acting like the music police; you won't win.

- Introduce them to your own music; maybe they'll love it later.

60

Wave the White Flag

*I*f you are the parent of a teen, you have likely engaged in conflict with them to some degree. You may even have instigated or inflamed it. No matter who started it, it's never too late to wave the white flag and initiate a round of family peace talks. Someone needs to step up to stop the yelling, door slamming, or silent treatment. Might as well be you!

Calling for peace is not glossing over incidents but acknowledging your part in the current conflict. "I was angry, and I insulted your character. I'm sorry." "I was tired, and I yelled at you. That wasn't fair." Asking for forgiveness is a huge step, but it's necessary to move on. Conflicts will come and go, but the relationship is forever. What your teen sees from you in the way of conflict resolution skills will shape their future interactions, as well.

*The only way we can
ever teach a child to say
"I'm sorry" is for him
to hear it from our lips first.*

KEVIN LEMAN

61

Know How to Handle the Movie Speech

Have you ever delivered a movie speech? You know, the one you mutter while you are scrolling through Netflix? "You have to be careful about what you see, it stays with you," or "We'll both have to agree on the movie content before we can watch it." My teens knew all the versions of the movie speech.

Then one day in their later teen years, I announced a new policy. The new speech went something like this: "I'm not going to give you the movie speech anymore. By now, I hope you understand my concerns. From now on, you can decide what's good for you to see and what's just a waste of an evening. I trust that you will choose wisely." I will never know all their choices, but there is a time to train and a time to trust.

62

Plan Table Talk

Decide in advance that dinnertime is off-limits for argument, confrontation, or criticism. Instead, look for opportunities to communicate, compliment, and celebrate. Avoid the familiar one-word answer, "fine," by being prepared for fun, interactive table talk. Here are some ideas to keep the talk flowing.

- Each person share something about their day—good or bad.
- Share something interesting that happened on this day in history.
- Ask about their favorite celebrity or sports team.
- Ask their opinion on current events. If it's different from yours, don't argue; just listen.
- Celebrate victories and accomplishments with a special dessert.

*There is more power
in a mother's hand
than in a king's scepter.*

BILLY SUNDAY

63

Say It Sideways

Few teens respond well to talking with their parents about sex, drugs, college, God, and other serious topics. You might find that sideways communication delivers the point just as well as a direct approach, without the confrontation factor. Try starting a hard conversation with a disclaimer: "You might need some time to respond, but here are my thoughts."

- Use something you have read or heard on the news as an opener.

- Reference an incident from your own teen years as an entry point.

- TV shows or movies can instigate great conversation.

- Start a discussion that includes their friends. A group dynamic may open things up. Be sensitive to private details, however.

- Post a meaningful quote on the bathroom mirror without commentary.

64

Try Not to Embarrass Your Teen

"Mom, can we look in your closet and pick out something for you to wear to parent-teacher conferences?" It was a sincere request from my seventh-grade daughter. Until your teen feels more secure in their own identity, anything you do feels like a reflection of them.

This subsides a bit later in adolescence, but until then, be sensitive to their high need not to be embarrassed. This might include talking too loud in public, "weird" questions or comments you make to strangers, grilling their friends on anything, behavior at sports events, or even PDA toward them. Of course, despite your best efforts, embarrassment will occasionally happen. Accept it for what it is and, once again remember, it's not about you; it's about them.

65

Teach Your Teen to Pray

....

Although you won't see much evidence of it on TV or in films, most of us are quite fluent in the universal language of prayer. When your teen was a child, you may have taught them to pray before bed, before meals, or as part of what you do in church. Those lessons are not over.

- Offer to pray for your teen's concerns— health, tests, tryouts, friends, etc.

- Remind your teen that prayer is a conversation that can be engaged in anytime, anywhere.

- If you don't usually pray before meals, start with a simple blessing. Don't be pushy on a particular style.

- Share your own experiences: "I really didn't know what to do, so I said a quick prayer."

*The impression that
a praying mother
leaves upon her children
is life-long.*

Dwight L. Moody

66

Touch Your Teen

....

Touch is important. Simply touching your teen can convey affection, comfort, connection, and support. If your teen has a tendency to pull away, there are still ways to touch that might be welcome.

- Offer a back rub when they flop down on the couch, or a shoulder massage while they're at the computer.

- Offer a quick hug for hellos and goodbyes, not a full embrace.

- Hold hands during meal prayer.

- While walking with your teen, slip your arm briefly around their waist or shoulders.

- If they are obviously stressed, ask if they need a hug.

67

Differentiate between Rules and Policies

Try fewer rules and more policies. A policy is flexible; a rule is fixed. Use policies for the minors of life such as room cleaning, late phone calls, attendance at family events, or established study times. A policy can be changed by request, "I need to talk to Sara tonight, but she won't be home till ten thirty. Can I call her later?"

Rules, however, cover the majors and are not flexible. There's simply no point in your teen asking if they can have a party when you're out of town. Likewise, there will be no exceptions as to whether they can drink and drive or have a sleepover with their boyfriend/girlfriend. Policies can be created on the spot and revised often, but the actual rules should be very few and very clear. Remember, rules without relationship can lead to rebellion.

A mother's love is patient and forgiving when all others are forsaking. It never fails or falters, even though the heart is breaking.

HELEN STEINER RICE

68

Speak Softly

....

When parents and teens live together, sooner or later, a voice will rise. Don't let it be yours. Dr. Mike Bradley, author of *Yes, Your Teen Is Crazy*, says that moms usually say too much while dads say too little in a conflict. Whatever you do say, say it softly. It is difficult to pick a fight with a pleasant voice.

The wisdom of Proverbs reminds us "a gentle answer turns away wrath, but a harsh word stirs up anger" (Proverbs 15:1 NIV). This is quite evident in conversations with teens. Practice some oft-used phrases to yourself in the mirror in a very quiet voice: "Tell me more about your plans." "Please explain what happened." "I need a little more information." "Before you go out, could you _____." Notice the difference in response. Adding a smile works well, too.

69

Enjoy Being a Mom

To enjoy being a mom, it is important to enjoy your teen. Ask yourself what it is that you enjoy about your teen. What about your relationship would you say really works? Of course, there will be things you wish were different, but it's important to start with what you enjoy and move forward from there.

Write those thoughts down, reflect on them, be thankful, focus on that good. If current circumstances are making this difficult, think back to what you used to enjoy and see if that is still there, beneath a few layers of teen angst. If you are really stuck, look back at baby pictures. They can renew your perspective quickly!

70

Keep Sight of the Three Tasks of Teens

You have probably already noticed that your teens are on a mission. That mission is programmed into their hearts and brains, and it's absolutely essential they succeed in it if they're to grow into healthy adults. And no, the mission is not to drive you crazy!

So what is the mission? You've already seen it in action.

- Identity: They must recognize their own strengths and sense of uniqueness.

- Inclusion: They must find a place of belonging in their peer group.

- Independence: They must begin making decisions for themselves.

These tasks must be completed to land well in life.

*For the mother is and must be,
whether she knows it or not,
the greatest, strongest,
and most lasting teacher
her children have.*

HANNAH WHITALL SMITH

71

Set the Stage

Remember trying to arrange time to hang out with someone you were interested in? Putting yourself at the right place at the right time? Clearing your schedule to be available "just in case"? Thinking about interesting things to talk about if you got the chance?

While great connections with our teens can sometimes just happen, setting the stage may be helpful. How do you do that?

- Be available in the common rooms of the house when they come home.

- Sit outside with an empty chair nearby to encourage them to join you.

- Give them your full attention, even when they've interrupted you.

- Have a few positive conversation bytes ready to start a friendly chat.

72

Encourage Your Teen to Get a Job

You're probably already shaking your head at your teen's schedule. Challenging classes, more homework than last year, extracurricular activities, youth group, time for the all-important hanging out with friends—enough already! Well, maybe not quite. When they are old enough, consider encouraging your teen to get a job.

Besides a taste of financial independence (they can pay for their own iTunes!), experts indicate that other benefits include increased confidence, better time management ability, and greater academic success. It's hard to argue with those results. Their first job may not lead to a career path, but the skills, connections, and experience may open doors later.

If we're always following
our children into the arena,
hushing the critics, and assuring
their victory, they'll never learn
that they have the ability
to dare greatly on their own.

BRENÉ BROWN

73

Ditch the Dread

....

"Wait till they're teenagers!" Oh, if only I had a nickel for every time I heard that foreboding warning—almost every time I took the stroller out. From the nursery to the playground to the boardroom, the mom-to-mom network bemoans the next step: wait till they learn to mouth off; wait till they reach high school; *just wait* till they get that driver's license! What are we waiting for? Why do we look for the worst?

Instead of lamenting the dire possibilities, start each day with a hope and a prayer that your teen is going to be okay. Talk back to your inner critic and tell her you're doing just fine as a mom. Don't let moments of doubt turn into dreadfests. Be the yea-sayer instead of the naysayer to other moms. Expect the best and wait for it to come!

74

Decide Instead of React

A mom's reaction response to an incident can take place in a flash. Sometimes it shows up in immediate declarations such as: "You're grounded!" or "Give me that phone!" or "You aren't driving for a long time!" In the moment, the words fly out.

While you might end up at any of those consequences, try to differentiate between a reaction and a decision. Tell your teen, "I feel really angry about what just happened. I need to sort this out." And then do.

If you need to do some backtracking, use that same language. "When I said you couldn't go to your game tonight, I was reacting, not deciding. You can go to the game, but you need to come home right after it is over." This response is not the same as "caving" but rather reflects a true decision instead of a reaction.

One Size Fits One

There are many conflicting positions out there. One parent will stick with a zero-tolerance policy—two minutes late for curfew and *slam!* Another will be softer, allowing for a twenty-minute grace period. You and your husband don't even agree on what is the best policy in certain situations. Who's right, anyway?

Remember toilet training? Discipline issues? Motivation rewards? You found the plan that worked for *your* toddler, not the one next door. Same goes for teens. What is the best plan for long-term success for your teen? Will a tight policy be the most effective, or does your teen respond better to a more grace-filled approach? There are a hundred right answers to your dilemma—but they all won't work for your teen. Know your teen. Know what works and what will most effectively correct that individual child.

Don't throw away your friendship with your teenager over behavior that has no great moral significance. There will be plenty of real issues that require you to stand like a rock.

JAMES C. DOBSON

76

How to Respond to "I Hate You!"

Many moms will hear the dreaded words, "I hate you," at some point, perhaps more often from early-teen daughters. What's the best response? First, let's look at what *not* to say:

- I hate you, too!

- You're grounded!

- You're just like your _____.

Instead, try to respond gently with something like: "I'm so sorry you feel that way. I love you so much" or "Before this goes any further, let's take a break."

Tears may come, but try to control them till you are alone. It's important to stay in charge and not throw fuel on the fire. Remember, this emotional outburst is much more about your teen than it is about you. Most kids, at some point, apologize.

77

Don't Fret about Their Room

Of course, you don't want your teen's room to be a health hazard, and it is frustrating to see those pricey clothes you bought piled up on the floor. But what is a reasonable standard of care that you can both agree to? Start with a conversation to find that out: "You and I have been having a lot of fights about your room. Can we see if we can work something out that doesn't get in the way of our relationship?"

Some hot topics to sort out are dishes, open food, wet towels, and who does the laundry. (Hey—there's a skill they need to learn!) Agree not to let an unmade bed come between you, but decide on standards you both can live with and then let go of the rest.

*The loveliest masterpiece
of the heart of God
is the love of a mother.*

SAINT THÉRESÈ OF LISIEUX

78

Is This a Good Time?

Maybe you need coffee before conversation, or maybe you don't function well after 9:00 p.m. You know what it takes to get you moving efficiently. Well, just like you, your teens have energy patterns. You can usually tell when they get out of bed, climb in the car, or walk in the door whether they are approachable. Try to work with their observable rhythms in hopes of getting a conversation, not just a grunt.

If you want to know plans, details, or updates, watch for a good time to ask. A tired, moody, hungry teen is not going to talk about anything enthusiastically. Wait until they've settled in or they've had a snack or dinner. Obviously, some conversations are urgent, but usually, asking yourself or your teen, "Is this a good time?" pays off in a much better answer.

79

Practice Good Self-Care

"If Mama ain't happy, ain't nobody happy." As moms of teens, it seems to work the other way, too. If our teen is out of sorts, we jump right in there with them. We allow ourselves to be consumed by their anxiety, frustration, and challenges—and we lose our center.

Here are some ways to hang on when
your teen is spinning out.

- Get out of the house; even a short drive can help.
- Take a night out with a girlfriend
  for dinner and a movie.
- Treat yourself to a haircut, manicure,
  facial, or some other self-care.
- Work out for an hour.
- Get lost in that novel you've been meaning to read.
- Pray for wisdom, endurance, and
  peace of mind and heart.
- Outline your personal goals apart from being a mom.

80

Be a Good Housemate

It's just fine to enjoy a simple housemate relationship with your teen. Find and enjoy those times when nothing profound needs to be said, no questions need to be asked, no chores need to be done, and the homework really is finished. It's easy to think of every quiet moment as an opportunity to have a memorable interaction, share a deep thought, or experience strong bonding.

If there's no connection spark as your teen walks through the room or sits down next to you on the couch, go ahead—keep reading your book, watching your show, drinking your tea. They probably just want to relax too. Feeling comfortable together is an initial step in all healthy relationships.

Being a mother is learning about strengths you didn't know you had and dealing with fears you never knew existed.

LINDA WOOTEN

81

Don't Be Afraid!

These days, watching the news, logging on to the internet, or even reading the paper can easily provoke anxiety. We long to protect our children from the things that seem to be lurking at the door. With so much violence in the news, how can we keep from being consumed by fear?

Even if it's not obvious, teens look to us to inform them how to react. Any freaking out we do will fuel their fear factor. The most important response might be to show courage, not fear.

Take precautions, do your research, but don't obsess. Being informed is empowering; being consumed is debilitating. It's important to remember that, while we cannot control what might happen, we can control how we respond, and that can make all the difference.

82

Ask for Volunteers

....

It won't matter much to your teen right now, but studies show that in sixty or seventy years, they will still be enjoying health benefits if they are active as volunteers now. Benefits reported include increased happiness and greater self-esteem. Volunteers report feeling more valued and enjoy learning new skills.

What is your role in this? Seventy-four percent of teenagers reported that their parents encouraged them to volunteer. A great way to do that is to let them see you doing so, as well. Invite them along and then step back to see what activities they choose for themselves. Most faith communities, hospitals, and park districts provide good opportunities for volunteers, or you could encourage an internet search for other opportunities in your area. Support what your teen chooses.

My mother was the making of me. She was so true, so sure of me; and I felt I had something to live for, someone I must not disappoint.

THOMAS A. EDISON

83

Give Them a Chore List

Household chores are everyone's responsibility, and expecting some help from your teens is quite reasonable. Three principles for chores that seem to work well are offering them choice, variety, and flexibility.

Choice involves just that: "This list is what we need to get done; what would you like to help with?"

For *variety*, divide responsibilities for different areas (the dog, the basement, bathroom, meal preparation, etc.), but set it up so the jobs change hands each month.

Flexibility means that major tests, tryouts, and events take priority over chores, so a trade or a pass can be requested and usually granted.

84

Offer a Second Chance

....

Instead of always pulling out the you're-grounded speech, try offering your teen second, third, or more chances to turn their behavior around. Responding with grace is most usually more effective than another weekend of being grounded.

When I blow it with my husband, kids, or friends, I hope they will give me a chance to try again. If I'm caught speeding, I'll be praying the officer gives me a warning ticket. Likewise, when I fall short spiritually, I trust God to forgive me as I forgive others.

Obviously, there are times and situations when a grounding of some sort is the wisest response, but when that is over or before it starts, be ready with the clean slate. There is power in love and grace and mercy and the resulting close relationship that grows from that.

85

Draw on Your Own Teen Years

On a recent visit to my hometown, I passed the old high school football stadium and vividly remembered walking into that arena full of angst. Was my jacket cool enough? My hair cooperating? Would I have anything to do after the game? The need to be *normal* yet *cool* was a constant pressure.

Your teen walks the halls of their school every day, wondering the same things. *Do I measure up? Am I too quiet/loud? Do I fit in yet stand out? Do I look/sound dumb? Am I noticed? Am I okay?* Take the time to remember the insecurity that most teens deal with most of the time, and reassure them they are just fine. You might *still* not feel like you have it all together, but one thing that is cool is to believe in your teen!

*All that I am
or ever hope to be,
I owe to my angel mother.*

ABRAHAM LINCOLN

86
Don't Turn Listening into a Lecture

When your teen confides in you or just makes an offhand comment, you have a choice to make—will you listen or lecture? Try to listen. I guarantee it will work better than a lecture. You can listen while doing several other tasks, but a better way is to practice "active listening." In this technique, the listener checks with the speaker to see that a statement has been correctly heard and understood. Clarify with, "I think this is what you're saying; is that right?" Great communication can result. Not so much with lectures.

Active listening usually leads to another conversation, while lecturing quite often leads to shutting down. Your teen will be more likely to listen to you when they feel you have heard them. Funny how saying less initially leads to talking more eventually!

87

Most Friends Are Passing Through

....

On a drive one day, I passed the home of a middle school friend of my daughter. I remember worrying at the time about whether that was a good relationship. Looking back, I'm sure it was just what my daughter needed at the time.

Most of your teen's friends will pass on through. Middle school friends don't often stick around past sophomore year, and the whole crowd usually changes by the end of high school. Adopt a wait-and-see policy with your teen's friends. As much as possible, avoid that wary attitude that's so easy to take. Trust that each friend is contributing something to the confident, competent adult your teen will be someday— even the ones you want to hurry along.

No matter their ages right now, no matter our age, this very minute as mothers, our hearts beat after our children.

JANE RUBIETTA

88

Involve Them in Holiday Planning

Give your teen ownership in the behind-the-scenes part of holiday celebrations by actively involving them in the planning. Let the artistic one design the family Christmas card. Ask the foodie's opinion on the menu for the special dinner or party; see what they would like to prepare. Is there a new driver who's still eager for a chance behind the wheel? Give them an errand list. Ask their input on ideas for gifts for younger siblings or cousins. They will remember what they liked at that age better than you do. Maybe the math genius can help prepare a holiday budget or the one with the lovely handwriting can address the cards.

Involvement means ownership. Your teen will have a larger holiday experience by being a part of the details.

89

Avoid Snooping

We are a society of voyeurs, and even our own teens' lives can seem fascinating or fearful. But, Mom, resist the urge to "just take a quick look" at their stuff. Whatever you find will not be worth the relationship damage if you're caught.

On the other hand, sometimes they leave notes lying around in public places or their computer open, almost inviting you to check it out. This might be your teen's way of inviting you into a situation where they feel overwhelmed. The obvious exception to the avoid-snooping rule is if you have evidence that your teen is struggling with life-or-death issues like drug use, illegal activity, or significant depression. In that case, do what you must to protect your teen.

90

Show Up for Their Events

Schools seem to pack the end of the year full of special programs. If your teen is involved in any extracurricular activity, you'll probably have some event to go to. Weary as you may be of one more run to the school, show up. Don't *just* show up, either. Grab the camera, buy the flowers, pick up the cake, and put on your happy face. You'll have plenty of time later for meetings, book clubs, and dinners with friends; your teen's event is now or never.

At these events, your teen might pay more attention to their friends and not notice how hard it was for you to get off work early. They might not be available to go out for ice cream afterward, but that's okay. They will remember that you came and cheered and clapped loudly . . . and that memory will count a lot.

Few things are more satisfying than seeing your own children have teenagers of their own.

DOUG LARSON

91

Change Your Parenting Style

....

You have probably figured out by now that what works to manage a four-year-old (you get to plan their time, choose their activities, select their playmates, and give time-outs) isn't effective with a fourteen-year-old. Or maybe even a twelve-year-old.

Changing your parenting style along the way while keeping your values is key to successful navigation of the teen years. What are some ways to do this?

- Blame less; bless more.

- Be available, but from a distance.

- Choose your battles; be willing to let go of the small stuff.

- Stop micromanaging.

- Gradually shift from instruction to influence.

92

Make Time for Your Marriage

Modeling a strong marriage is one of the best things you can do for your teen. Make your marriage a priority. How?

- Take advantage of early morning time to take a walk, go out for coffee or breakfast, or snuggle in bed.

- Be willing to say no to the kids and yes to your spouse.

- Agree not to talk about the kids on a date.

- Schedule your dates in advance and look for new things to do—a restaurant, a biking path, a live performance.

- Despite being tired or wondering if you can afford to go out, know that your marriage is worth the effort. Stay invested!

A woman who fears the LORD will be greatly praised.

PROVERBS 31:30 NLT

93

Allow a Few Mental Health Days

....

"Mom, can I stay home?" Most teens will occasionally want to stay home from school. Here are some principles on when to allow a mental health day.

- Your teen has completed the tests or projects he's been cramming for.

- Your teen is in a social crisis, and space might help.

- You can spend the day with your teen doing something fun.

- Your teen is clearly exhausted.

Never lie to the school when you call in; say your teen is staying home for personal reasons that you've approved.

94

Be Their Source

Have you noticed how your source becomes your authority? When new information is acquired, we'll often return to that source for clarification, more details, or questions. Sources can include friends, books, teachers, even the internet. Choose to be your child's first source. If there's something valuable you want them to know, tell them yourself before someone else does.

This is especially important with sex education, as there are many sources of available information on that topic, and many of them are sketchy to say the least. Many good resources exist to help you with this if you are uncomfortable, but don't let someone or something else become the authority.

95

Make Room For Dad

There's not much debate about the value of a dad spending more time with his teen son or daughter. So how can you encourage your spouse to find the time to connect in an already-demanding schedule?

- When the two of them are talking to each other, step out of the picture.

- Ask Dad to handle some of the driving involved in getting your teen around.

- Support plans they make together, even if it means more work for you.

- Offer suggestions, if needed, for fun ways for them to connect on the weekend.

- Don't expect Dad to do everything the way you would—and be okay with that.

Praise the developing character in your child as it emerges in active, loving, responsible behavior.

HENRY CLOUD

96

Celebrate Anything

....

For over forty years, my family has celebrated the first day of spring (March 20) with a picnic. Rain or snow, outside or inside, the picnic happens. Whatever was going on with our teens was suspended by buffalo wings, lemonade, deviled eggs, and goofy fun. No doubt this worked because they were born into this tradition and—despite the embarrassment of being seen anywhere with us, especially on a picnic in March—the family bonding worked.

Celebrate anything; celebrate often! Invite family members by text, Snapchat, signs on the fridge, or notes on the pillow. Good grades, passed tests, NCAA basketball victories, half-birthdays, dog birthdays—all are possibilities for special desserts, impromptu speeches, and fun times.

97

Trick or Treat is for Teens Too

We may think of it as a child's activity, but many teens still enjoy trick-or-treating. It gives them a chance to kick back and be a kid again for an evening, not to mention the piles of candy they'll score.

If your teen wants to head out, what are some guidelines?

- Ask the usual questions: who's going; where are you headed?

- Send them out with a laugh and a kiss.

- Take photos and be sure to give them some of your candy stash too.

Even if you do think the idea of teens trick-or-treating is crazy, in the spirit of choosing your battles, this one is minor. Let it go.

98

Be Yourself

....

We quickly undermine ourselves when we start comparing ourselves with other moms: *If only I were more fun like* _____, *more patient like* _____, *had wisdom like* _____. While wanting to do and be the best mom we can be is a good desire, strive to be the best version of yourself, not some other mom that your teen knows. With all of your foibles and quirks, you bring to your family a unique style that is just what they need. Your teen may like the way other moms do things, but you're the one they love.

The days are long,
but the years are short.

GRETCHEN RUBIN

99

Carry on the Tradition

The day after Thanksgiving found us once again at the tree farm, bow saw in hand. Our adult kids and their families joined us as they introduced this time-honored ritual to our grandchildren. The tradition has survived the I-don't-want-to-be-with-my-parents stage, the I'd-rather-be-shopping stage, and the "aren't-they-cheaper-at-Home-Depot" stage; it now is a holiday favorite for everyone.

Family traditions provide identity and stability for each member of your clan. Weather the storm of skepticism about the value of the tradition and proceed as usual. We've dropped some traditions and added a new ones now and then, so all is not set in stone. When you start hearing, "When are we going to . . ." in reference to a tradition, you'll know it's a keeper.

100

Resolve to Reconnect after the Holidays

One New Year's resolution you could make is to reconnect with your teen in a meaningful way after the holidays are over, when school resumes and the many family events are finished. Try one or more of these activities:

- Spend some time together at your favorite coffee shop, relaxing and reminiscing.

- Head out to that blockbuster movie you missed in the holiday rush.

- Write a personal love note and leave it in their room.

- Take a mug of cocoa to their room during a study time.

- Start daydreaming with them about summer options.

About the Author

Letitia Suk is a retreat leader, speaker, personal life coach, blogger (www.hopeforthebest.org), and the author of *Getaway with God* and *Rhythms of Renewal*. She and her husband, Tom, a marriage and family therapist, live in the Chicago area and are the parents of four grown children.